Notes from the Girl Cave

Notes from the Girl Cave

Poems by

Sarah Carleton

Cover DESIGN BY Shay Culligan

ISBN: 978-1-950462-75-9

Kelsay Books Inc.

kelsaybooks.com

502 S 1040 E, A119
American Fork, Utah 84003

To my husband and best friend, Phil Levy

Acknowledgments

Avatar Review (Issue 18): "Sing to Me of Florida Summers"

Avatar Review (Issue 15): "Alchemy"

Cider Press Review: "Falling Hard," "Lost"

Ekphrastic: "Bathsheba," "Come Spend Summer in the Girl Cave"

Homestead Review (Fall 2015): "Acoustic Neuroma in the Family," "That Photo," "Waiting"

Houseboat: "The Flags of Women," "Travel," "Asafetida and Ginger" "Camping with Quilts"

Kindred (2016): "New Orleans Hosts a History Conference"

New Ohio Review (Fall 2017): "Here Below"

Nimrod (Fall 2015): "Orchard Orb-Weaver"

Off the Coast (Spring 2014): "Off-Season"

Off the Coast (Summer 2015): "Ithaca, NY," "Cinders"

Off the Coast (Summer 2016): "Poem or Pheasant"

Peacock Journal (December 2018): "Blue Came by Night," "Surprise Visit," "Invasive"

Pirene's Fountain (Spring, 2020): "Miami Airport Nocturne"

Poetry Quarterly (Fall 2015): "Queen and Jacks"

Poetry Quarterly (Summer 2013): "Daffodils in February"

Poetry Quarterly (Winter 2015): "Tall Windows"

Rise Up Review: "Seventy-Percent Occlusion"

Shark Reef (Issue 24, Summer 2014): "Stir Crazy"

Shark Reef (Issue 31, Winter 2018): "Nesting"

Sheila-Na-Gig (Volume 2.2, Winter 2017): "Tropical Wanderer"

Shot Glass Journal: "Art and Nature," "Before waking"

Silver Birch (October 2015): "The Have Nots"

Spillway (24, June 2016): "Cat and the Woodpile"

Tar River Poetry (2017): "Souvenir from a Windy Planet"

The Binnacle (2015): "Bollywood Diva"

The Binnacle (2016): "If you can read this"

The Binnacle (2017): "Memory"

The Chattahoochee Review (Fall 2015): "At the Smoothie Booth"

The Offbeat (Vol. 18, Spring 2018): "Far from Home"

Wild Violet (Summer-Fall 2014): "Learning to Mourn," "Rachel"
   "Flying Tortoise"

Contents

Part I: She

Poem or Pheasant

A poem is a pheasant.
   —Wallace Stevens

I poached one, hauled it home in a linen bag,
recognizing it as that fowl of old novels,
hybrid of *peasant* and *pleasant* and *feh*.

It was camouflaged in self-awareness and sensory detail,
a nutritious meal wrapped in babble.
I rousted it then vowed to set twenty more

loose in my backyard to dash
across the grass and burp out trills
while my bard's heart beat alliteration and floating feathers.

I planned a fence so high the flock would have to stay put,
since life without them would be a scrappy landscape
pocked with armadillo holes.

You know how this ends—
with the gate left open and the feudal phrases flown.
Oh, poetry, be my bird untrapped, my strut in the forest;
show me how far you can roam.

Off-Season

On the bus to Kinsale you meet a woman
who mistakes you for a Botticelli goddess.

She speaks in civilized syllables, her words
like calico (evenly printed, well ironed).

You rumple the landscape and she follows—
anchoring her city socks ankle-deep in mud,

scraping corduroys thin on the walls of ruins.
She stands with you against angles of downpour

and surveys the coast. Towards evening,
the illusions snag on a boulder

and high tide washes them away.
You are human; she is bedraggled;

the conversation is soggy and full of old salt.
You sit with her in a cold room

and attempt to mend your brocade.
Two pairs of leather shoes block the space heater,

forcing you both to flannel and warm sheets.
The shoes bake all night.

By the time you wake up they are brittle.

Cinders

I tapped a keg of tears and flooded the town.
He said, *No woman no cry.* It made me cry harder.
I held his empty shirt to my face at night

and breathed in tobacco, sweat and woodsmoke
till I fell into heartsick sleep in my unheated attic
and woke to piles of dead flies on the window sill.

Once upon a few weeks earlier, we met at the dance
and spied seven deer in a field of snow,
which he proclaimed magical.

He grew strange after that, but cats crossed the street
to greet me. Thrift-store dresses fit. My shoes felt seamless.
I stayed out way past midnight, propelled by music—

until the spring thaw. Let's skip to the part
where grief gives way to a recurring dream
of finding a whole other house behind my mirror.

I swept away the flies, went downstairs
and sat happily evermore by the fire with my girlfriends,
cracking jokes dirty as creosote burning in a stove pipe.

Falling Hard

Never mind the grand green vistas,
the granite-walled highways,

the crunch of tires on a dusty dirt road.
Forget the wild blackberries lining the path,

the clumps of brown pine needles
separating each blade of grass

and don't get attached to knobby purple hollyhocks
and fat, spotted chickens,

the clean, hot scent of Queen Anne's lace
in the morning, the loon cry at midnight—

in just a few months, you'll don your down booties
and hide in the house till your neighbor

plows the driveway;
you'll watch the woodpile shrink

and calculate splits like a bank balance.
You'll wake with your fleece cap already on,

wrap your hands around a burning ceramic mug
and think bitterly of summer, that serial enchantress.

And when the room has finally warmed up, you'll smell
fresh cold leaking in from the edges of the window

and you'll glance out through the glass and fall hard—
for dead weeds in refrozen snow,

for stunted skies and half-light broken by skeletal branches
and for all that artless blight.

If you can read this

you're too close, so take a step back.
I do the swing-arm warmup.

I do the warrior pose.
I like to roll tight like a tamale

or snap wide open like a multi-tool.
Even my similes are unpredictable.

Leave a buffer, you read me?
The open book that's me reads,

Scram, or make me laugh.

Bollywood Diva

She in lime green and magenta
parts the sea of men, a bright flash

of sari scarf against their cryptic poses.
Her arms sweep their breath aside;

she flirts with the wind and leads the drab
backdrop crowd around the marketplace,

making them shift and shift again, like
mistress to a school of fish.

She is all the dances they suppress:
torque and wiggle, finger to the chin,

skip and two-step, hip and head
rotation, rolling eyes, wild spin, meadow

chase. She even thwacks a cricket ball
for them and, when they stand,

jigs their victory.

Come Spend Summer in the Girl Cave

Plunk your pencils in vases,
hang kimonos on nails,
paint tired things glossy
coral and red. Let your secrets
swell like a rising sun

and repurpose your lies.
Bring scones, coffee;
whine and be messy—
throw capes on carpets;
leave rings on tables.

Wear dresses that drape and
poof in the wind—
like that sea-foam muumuu
your husband hates—
or wear nothing at all.

Get rid of your shoes
and lead with your toes;
settle in.
You'll be camouflaged here
among the round pitchers,

floral blankets and nudes.
We'll doodle dancers,
sort buttons, tear magazine
pictures, pose for each other
or just zone out and eat jam.

Surprise Visit

My mom surrounds herself with color—
Oaxacan animals, quilts, rugs woven from bright double-knit rags,

and her own watercolors, which can make a pile of grocery bags
look like the lifestyle you long for.

New Englanders shift in their graves
to see her centuries-old house painted yellow.

She's found a new way to wear the ruffle scarf I knitted
—flattened out over her narrow shoulders like a rosy cape—

and she keeps forty birthdays' worth of funky earrings
displayed on the dresser year-round in case we suddenly show up.

At eighty, she still heats with beauty.
We give her gifts just to see her glow.

My mom's surprise is as vivid as a sunrise
when the four of us rap on her door one night in February,

our toes burning from the cold.
Her "Oh!" goes through shades of joy

like paint cards fanning magenta to orange.

Daffodils in February

On leap day came rain and mud
and swaths of daffodils

on the forest floor. Long before
the season of languid heat set in

to grease my shoulders with sweat,
I ran before dawn like a night-horse,

darkness erasing my weight
and gravity. I flew to road's end

and over the black ribbon of
trodden dirt leading down to the river.

Thirty-some-odd years ago, suspended
in the sky, I said,

Remember this moment,
and even saying that, leapt beyond

the moment to my now-self remembering.
I told myself,

This morning is perfect,
but in thus speaking had to nullify

a hundred numb teenage nights
recorded in a journal.

I crinkle the page. Empirical memory,
graceless and hard-shelled,

crumples into ecstatic flight.
My quick breath fills the pockets

between footfalls. I dash through
the yellow-spangled ground cover

to the log that spans the water
and cross over at a canter,

aware that I could easily tumble,
knowing that I won't.

Bathsheba

Blame it on the desert air
that drew the moisture off her like a slip

or the moon that spotlit her hair
and the creases under each ass cheek

or the power of a glimpse of sponge
on crook and fold and dimple.

Once watching, he could no more let the ritual be
than leave a psalm

half-composed.
Even the rug's roughness, the cold of stone

weren't hers to own in the city of a king.
So he trained his focus on her skin,

ignoring the flat rooftops beyond, and self-doubt
lay under wraps

like the curve of a waist beneath a kaftan.

Acoustic Neuroma in the Family

She who can tuck
her foot behind her neck,
walk on her hands,
carve thirty pumpkins in one sitting,
grow happy sons and pick
plump peas in summer
has gone to California.

She gave us signs—
a hand braced on the counter,
stacks of unread library books,
a sudden absence of sarcasm,
ramped-up volume, naps.

Now she shuffles around a hospital
with a gauze-banded bump on her head,
while back home apples pucker
and water sours.
Children whine in tongues.
Walls expand; corners go missing.
Silence wraps me
like an oversized turban

and sound waves dissolve at my feet.
I close my eyes against a stumble
and imagine her standing
in a berry-stained dress,
brown hair smooth behind her ear,
and my heart so open
it spills light onto her
as I fall.

Part II: Drumbeats

Orchard Orb-Weaver

Having strung one orb she felt compelled
to waltz concentric rings around it, ripple

the gap between broad leaf and blossom, weave
a curtain out of air. Backdrop done,

she rappelled on silk to a spot in the sun and posed
against the grid, a glint on a drape,

red-specked and yellow-flecked abdomen
making me recoil quickly.

Hourglass-marked or not, she had to be a widow
or recluse or poet or hacker

or some other dangerous loner—
or so I figured, forgetting that bright women

merit an Internet search, not a panicked squashing.
I who spent hours humming at the sewing machine,

cutting circles of velveteen, pinning strips of piping,
tore my own karmic fabric when I leaned into the ginger plant

and clapped the pretty artist between two boards.
Only after did I check the web and learn her name

and the harmlessness of her venom. Now I've lost my thread;
the tension is wrong and the stitches bunch

and I question my craftsmanship. In public, I'm wary of glistening;
I won't wear a bold print when I go out dancing.

Art and Nature

He's plugged in so only he can hear
and he paints by playing, letting guitar chords splat
on a purple background like vertical birds flying
in a line across the computer screen,

wings spread for sustained notes, blank spaces
for pockets in between—bird, space, bird, space,
regular as planted rows.

Outside, weed sparrows flit down from a low branch
and search the ground for chicken feed,
with the squeaks and fight squawks
of the feral. They flap rapid and hop like fluff.

I borrow an earbud and watch him sow a riff.
I'm waiting for a flock to sprout—
for notes to lift off, scatter and soar.

The Have Nots

It was the summer we played that X song
from New York to Virginia

and all the way back, Blue Ridge to Finger Lakes,
highway zooming through the bass lines,

exits flashing between riffs,
you and I wailing out words, ready for the moment

E-minor to B no longer made our skin hum
—which never came—foot heavy on the gas pedal

when percussive joy struck
whoever was driving while the other person

stared out the window at the bittersweet world,
letting pun-laden bar names and signs for Scranton

patch into a single story
of two twenty-somethings coursing through decade

after decade till today, while I stir
the tomato sauce and listen

to you on the couch, figuring out the chords,
our hearts beat road trip.

Here Below

Before a careless bulldozer buried him under a ton of dirt
he played with impeccable pulse.
He anchored tunes with a standup bass,

left fingers spidering, right hand patting pauses,
a running commentary that thumped below the chitchat,
bristling with off-color intent.

Just as hothouse plants rooted and swelled
to his sweet, muttered, nasty guy's-guy nothings,
we set our feet in the soil of his crude jokes and thrived.

His wife didn't pay much mind to the dirty stories
and sly non-secrets. When he laid their deck,
he penciled women's names on the underside of the planking,

like an ode to abundance, and she just laughed, shrugging.
We take our cue from her and refuse to fret,
but celebrate him in smut and subtext.

Without crawling among the snakes to check, we hope
we made the list—divas of warm skin and rayon dresses
immortalized on a two-by-ten—

and we also aspire to be like his wife,
who stands aboveboard, rolling her eyes, knowing
her name has been etched more than once in that slatted dark.

The Flags of Women

Back then she rejected pink
but welcomed the desert
with its packed, rocky dirt,
silver sagebrush and creosote.
While the fiddler drove, she watched
low-built subdivisions thin to single houses
and blend into scrub.
At each territory, laundry lines
stood at full mast,
waving bubblegum sports bras,
nighties and drawstring pants—
the flags of women.

Later onstage, she plunked a salute
to the colors of her sex, hooking
clumsily into the fiddler's jaunty bowing.
She admired how skirts on the dance floor
twisted from partner to partner as the ladies
stomped and spun and how
at the end, the dancers filed out the door
with flushed cheeks,
covered dishes hugged to their bellies.

The drive home offered no fluttering banners.
Midnight's landscape was roadside bushes
looming in headlamps and inky slopes.
Her nostrils itched. It began to rain,
smearing the dust on the windshield.
You've got to smell this, he said
when the sprinkle let up.
He pulled over and she followed him

out of the car, tiptoeing between needles
and shadows, deep into the plain.
Silence rinsed the last remnants of music
from her eardrums.
Water molecules hung in the air,
rousing stones and cactus buds.
She sniffed the musty lemon scent
and didn't want to move—
come daybreak, the prickly pears
would burst with rosy bloom.

Part III: Cave Paintings

Invasive

For the wild petunias, it's always party time.
New blossoms appear each day.
They never run out of purple.

Breezy, arms raised, lightly planted,
they spread like cheerful children in a park
but yank out easily when it's time to weed.

Troupes of them perform for hurricanes,
modern dancers swaying
and bending en masse

till the sun comes back out
and that pool of stuck rainwater's
a beauty bath that makes them brighter.

I confess I invited these flowers—
they're easy guests, an unsinkable
raft of bloom amid the mess.

That Photo

Twenty years ago, your smile took up the whole picture,
broad and wicked below your shaved head,
bold light bleaching your pen-scrawled T-shirt, and the dead
bird an inexplicable prop hanging between two hands.

Your grin, midpoint like the v in "devil,"
pushed from chin to ears,
at gleeful odds with the ragged owl
you stretched open like a grim cut-paper project.

I used to search the thin face for signs of you,
finding one top-center skewed tooth
that held you in place in the hard-edged black and white.

I saw the bird and its frayed-wing shadow as wildlife
that far predated our first bear hug,
but lately time and you have contracted:

you crouch by the road—very nearly my sweetheart—
while upstate rises behind and around like a vast
hammock of land that holds you for me.

Queen and Jacks

You will have your living-room fury
and I my Friday supper.

You'll set dice under bare feet
and I round bowls on a square table.

You'll conjure pillows trailing fluff,
cracked pen caps and 52-card pickup,

and I a linen runner with red roosters and yellow flowers
bright as a wedding day in 1992.

You'll scatter shoes and fold books backward
while I plant forks and spoons.

You'll leave keyboards sticky, paper torn,
flashlights open, quilt beasts on the floor;

I'll leave phones charged, candles upright,
bookmarks wedged, countertops wiped,

and then we'll have dry towels and rose soap,
jasmine rice steaming, potatoes roasted,

plates counted, lettuce spun, glasses filled,
bedlam on pause and washed hands.

Rachel

All night you dream of Rachel:
her half-fisted fingers and pimpled cheeks,
her sticky new lashes, her flannel-heavy bottom
in the crook of your arm
muttering the morning's mess.
Her mouth round as a fish's,
searching for a nipple in her sleep.

Eyes blink, ears blush,
day's first pink flush touches the room
and you, who measured the night by infant cries,
now turn to feed her
the moon, breast milk, a fleet of years,
as she feeds you
the tyranny of her sweetness.

At the Smoothie Booth

Clumps of bees kiss the honey jug.
Scores of them pile on pineapple slices,
hover in scent, stick to juicy surfaces,
pitch a hum just below bliss.

I trust the thick buzz I rest on
even when the blender drowns it out.
I stay and watch and sip my smoothie—
with ginger, for a little sting.

He tightens the top with fruit-soaked fingers,
looks at me with his patch-free eye,
says, *They'll push the lid off if you let them—*
and they do, nuzzling the screw thread

with tiny bee hands, abuzz with honey lust.
Scooping berries through the swarm,
he tells me, *Bees love organic.*
Everywhere I go, the bees come to me.

In a nearby field, colonies hide
behind shimmer and daze.
Soon they'll mill into view and fly this way,
dense as a flock of starlings.

Flying Tortoise

My son can tell turtle from tortoise
and this one's the latter,
breast-stroking half-webbed arms through the air while
sailing forward, held in small hands

that carry the critter like a messy hamburger
(fingers on the underside, thumbs on hexagons,
elbows angled). The tortoise's tough reptilian arms
curve, sweep and retract, dry-swimming

as we airlift him from parking lot to forest.
We laugh at the audacity of his black bullet head,
which he stretches out front like a curious tourist.
"He likes me," says Felix,
setting him carefully down in a puddle.
"Animals always like me."

Alchemy

She loved palmetto bugs,
medjool dates with legs that wiggled,
a treat gobbled between cracked corn
and milo.
She overturned plastic cups
in search of snacks we captured
just for her. Split-second beak darting,
roaches disappeared with a jerk.

Then with plowshares alchemy
her body turned crawling things
into brown eggs for our breakfast;

grains and grasses, too, remixed
inside the same hot belly
that pressed into the palm of my hand
when I held her to calm
her cackled complaints,

stroking the jewel-black
feathers of her neck
just to feel the squawk subside to a gurgle.

We eat neither fowl nor hemiptera
but some omnivore made a meal
of our darling, ravaged her plump gleam
to a grimy dishrag,

dug a moon out of her middle
so that she hung in concave
segments from my husband's hands

with her premature egg left in the grass
a few paces away
translucent and white as an angel.

Cat and the Woodpile

Crescent's the queen of the woodpile,
ascending logs with a beam-light
feline stride and basking.

In autumn everything spills and falls
except her highness:
witch-hazel leaves fill with yellow fire
and drop, acorns plummet,
walnuts scatter and lodge between
chunks of unstacked elm and beech,
chipping the mound of hardwood
into further erosion.

Crescent glories in the disorder
and over-ripeness of her terrain.
She rolls on a whisker-thin network of cobwebs,
licking dry leaves from between her toes;
she lolls on invisible shawls,
passing moles from paw to paw;
she strolls from shadow to shadow,
pissing on the edges of winter.

Learning to Mourn

Dirty fingers part the nylon nest
and search for life,
stroke a pair of minute spines,
checking the damp, unfeathered skin
for signs of breathing.
The jays lie lumped together, pink and raw,
wet dog food wedged in their beaks.

This time last year my son waded in the bay
with a busload of first graders,
gathering crab casings, gooey fish and
bright shells in buckets,
all floating and splashing in the sun,
while we parents stood knee-deep
and absentmindedly watched the shallows
for submerged heads and floundering limbs,

aware of the forces that drag children under,
that led two classmates
to a trailer where a man with tiny pupils
picked them apart like dark meat.

A year ago my son peeled off
his salty swaddling clothes
and spat at sorrow, vowed revenge,
strutted bravado, kicked our shins.
Now he weeps for his wee bird babes,
tosses dirt, reads aloud my bookmarked verse,
and redirects his gaze to the mountains.

Nesting

The mouse in our house is a rat,
lugging stale pita across the floor
like a shield,

slipping inside the stove
all scramble and scratch,
ignoring our Havahart trap.

She's a cookie-crumb snatcher,
a crack-of-dawn raider,
a mad-rodent hausfrau,

a twisted bedmaker who
turns art to confetti
and scatters scat in fabric,

that shred-happy
ghost of nested futures
sent to gnaw our drywall to dust.

Waiting

At the rental-car lobby, the toddler climbs
on her mama like crawling into bed,
sobs and sobs, but her mama says
No. You can't always have the thing you want.
Don't be extra.

The room has no toys, TV, books, colors,
smells, myths or curves.
It demands extra. I knit to fill the space,
looping blue yarn over thin metal needles,
building arcs of lace.

The van finally fetches us, driven by
a bright-eyed guy in khakis.
I stow my knitting. The mama dozes.
Little one from her car seat watches
neighborhoods roll by.

I stock the silence with speculation. The driver
is from Tallahassee. He answers questions
but never poses them. The tattoo on his forearm
says *You only live once* in fancy script.
My arms are blank pages.

Sing to Me of Florida Summers

Go. Dash from house to car, from car
to house, dodging mosquitoes while receipts

escape your pockets. Once safe inside your cool box,
count bites while entropy washes over the forlorn half acre

and tropical rainstorms fill the backyard like a tub,
piquing savage weeds that creep through grass.

A shawl of moths shakes lace over the pond
you used to call a lawn. Wear gumboots

to protect your feet from surprises, and shun
the cat-sized toad who croaks beneath the hibiscus

then disappears when puddles drain to sticky mud.
Here comes the unbearable sun, thunder at three,

the daily downpour, steam bursting and making
more steam. Forget the swimming pool;

no one goes there anymore. Deep in the season,
potato vines creep through sealed windows,

anoles leap on screens and streets burn empty.
Look around you. The party's over, marked by wild

and human litter: mashed acorns
with oily trails, shredded wrappers,

shovels gone rusty. Count one newspaper
for every week since June, plastic baggies

stuck to the ground in spoonfuls of grey mush.
This is their home now.

Stir Crazy

Eight days of rain and he's climbing the door jambs,
bare feet and spine wedged against the molding,
clothing strewn below.
He inches up: Mommy, look at me!

Going out doesn't help.
The grocery store makes him rage—
ten aisles, thirty-six kinds of gum,
and the registers beep! Beep! Beep!

Day nine, we hike under a hot grey sky,
brushing against poison ivy and teenagers.
It's the rainforest, a jungle full of spies.

We cross a stone wall that dams
green bottles, logs, stagnant algae,
sticks and crunched cans.
On the drop-down side it lets loose
a pounding muddy gush.

We edge past a guy with a nylon line
and a wiggly fish. Dodging bombs, we dash
around plastic bags, berry-bush prickles,
coffee-cup jackets and crane poop.

My son runs ahead. The path widens,
and the roar I thought was traffic
turns out to be the river—crashing rapid,
brown, smashing the edges off of boulders,
so deafening and angry it calms him.
He watches.

Blue Came by Night

He painted puffy cumuli
flat bottomed in a sage-colored sky.

Orange enthralled him during the day
with spirals of swirling speckles;

tones of grey made head shots,
pocked iron and oil spills.

Sly yellow ochre impersonated gold,
crimson splashed and sashayed

and all shades came finally
to spatter-paint the kitchen. Careless,

he left the evidence—brown on the pans,
vermillion on the dish towels,

violet on the teapots, cadmium on the cabinets,
green on the linoleum floor.

Late afternoon, his palette bled
pigment into the sink—

afterglow of many hues—
but blue waited till nighttime

and kept him up till long past
the hour when the bats tucked in.

He caught cornflower jewels,
cerulean fish, sapphire bubbles,

indanthrene shadows. Cobalt globes
rounded his ragged edges.

He had pthalo for oceans of well-being
and navy to call forth a starry sleep.

True, he remembered to clean his brushes,
but when I awoke to streaming sun

I found clues in the drain basket:
watery strands of blue.

Part IV: Dream Walk

Asafetida and Ginger

You say potato and I say aaloo
and you say hungry and I say poori.
So you say colonialism
and I say basmati steam.
You say, crispy dosa dipped in sambar?
and I say bingo.
I say wood block.
We're talking about textiles again,
and you say scrawny children with fingers needle-sore.
I say the rough feel of hand-printed cotton,
the waxy smell, the floating paisleys.
Remember that skirt with the elephants?
You say no and I say trunk-to-tail along the edge?
You say teabagger logo.
I say they don't have those people in India.
I say primeval seven-ton beast.
You say, let's free her from their lapel pins.
I say pass the chutney.
I say let's cut her ground-shaking self loose
from curtain borders and Babar books;
let's let her crawl out of stone walls.

Before waking

we packed up the miniature squirrels
except the one that scrambled onto the roof—

or maybe they were goats. I saw them jumping
when I went to clear out the A-frame—

or maybe it was a lean-to. The guy called it a tent.
He said he met a fundraising group

camping in the forest out back, but maybe
it was a role-play group bounding through the woods

with Robin Hood bows and arrows.
They called themselves the Gold

and when I turned to search for them
between the tree trunks, the forest shifted yellow.

Bright leaves shivered onto brown-green branches
and filled the frame. The ground was a mattress of mulch.

He said "We have to go now," but I wasn't sure.
Maybe I wanted to stay and sleep in golden leaves.

Road to Almost

This is not the long road you walked as a child
but the one you've been dreaming about ever since.

A treehouse in New England rises next to an alley in Dublin
two hills away from the French Revolution.

You might bypass metered parking,
cut through a mountain lodge and step into an event

under a big-top tent that reeks of deodorant and gin.
You might hike past a pink trailer and a cow named Lily

and wander into a field of phlox and musicians.
The map keeps changing, and the destination is moot.

Your few encounters never get past small talk—
two beats after "hello," you roll away like water off a tarp

and land in a different party.
After years of meandering, you finally locate nighttime

at the bottom of a dead-end street, leaking ink onto a porch.
Before you know it, you're dipping carrot sticks

in the kitchen with the wary ones
and watching a man through the archway.

When his partner disappears, you'll try to snag him,
but he'll always be in another room.

Fourth of July

Oh say, we saw the neighborhood
fill with sulfur smoke like a nocturnal
reenactors' camp. I breathed the weird brew

and summoned waistcoats, hardtack, smelly wool.
My son, an avid time traveler too, watched light
exploding behind the trees. From somewhere past

the backyard, we heard troops of voices stumbling,
so I grabbed keys, and we went on a reconnaissance
stroll through the muddled dark to the next street over

where people gathered on a lawn—
not soot-faced revolutionary soldiers
but sleeveless women raising drinks and sparklers

round a guy who juggled fire-lit clubs.
Applause burst in air. Reflectors gleamed red
and from the carport shone a cat's yellow glare.

Miami Airport Nocturne

These places are always so hushed.
Even that child bouncing from chair to chair

makes subsonic waves. His parents open their mouths
and release undetectable scolding into the tank.

Spanish sounds like bird chatter
in the pocket of a wool coat,

the middle range tamped down. Suitcases roll, roll
without a hitch on endless terrazzo mirrors.

The lack of definition stupefies. I dream open-eyed
until a group of women draped in yellow

salwar kameez and headscarves
shine their excitement at the arrivals gate.

Lost

In the night, in the wind, I search the roadside
for white feathers glued to a leather mask,

but the weeds and burrs won't give up their secrets
and my neck hurts from looking down.

Traffic shoves a gust—
a plastic bag fills with air and floats away

and for a minute I think it's my chiffon scarf
that disappeared in 1982.

I have reached the highway of lost things.
I'm keeping a lookout for odd screws,

rosin, milkweed fluff, embroidery needles,
senile cats, sharks' teeth and a straw hat

that blew off at the beach twenty years ago
and could have washed up, waterlogged,

to lie in limbo among iPods, sock mates,
habits, infatuations, flight phobia and muscle tone.

When my eyes adjust to the dark, I expect
to find it all here on the berm, stuck in the prickles.

Tall Windows

I.

It's raining where I work,
nearly snowing, pouring slush.
Road water under truck tires
wiggles like old glass.
These tall windows make the world
look wet even on dry days.
Yesterday they made the goldenrod
house across the street
look like a puddle of fire.

II.

Some things mutate
under glass and water, like
Julia, lacquered in oil
at the beach, submerged between
surface water and reef,
then shooting out slippery,
splitting in pieces
like several fish swimming together.

III.

The ladies like my silver woven-salt
damp silk sweater.
They say I seem like pewter undersea.

All the Winds

Here all the winds let go sooner or later, all of them.
—Pablo Neruda

One knocks trashcans over;
the next roars for days and throws the bay onto the city.
Tornados hit randomly. The jet stream is off its rocker.

Low currents puff my shirt when I hold still.
The gulf sighs and sighs, and a sidelong
chuff smacks my cheek.

Each house, too, has a bag of wind,
doors opening to free the squabbles.
If we shout outside, will the bluster harmonize us?

The air's a mosh pit of squalls
and the sky is curled with Van Gogh stirrings.
I want to stand by the water with my ears open
and be tossed like orange blossoms loosening.

Seventy-Percent Occlusion

Moonlight poured into sunlight
and dyed the grass Kodachrome green.
The neighborhood went quiet as a postcard.

Ranch-house yards stood empty,
shadows pointing farther than midday,
branches inking along the width of the street.

We sat on the dock and sweated and waited.
The water, black and still as onyx,
was pressed between banks of weeds two feet high,

overfed by fertilizer runoff.
Alligators thought a storm was brewing
and settled on the river bottom, out of sight.

The sky blinked and went periwinkle.
In broad eerie daylight, we blocked thoughts
of silhouettes lurking at government windows,

armed men oozing through familiar streets,
bodies flying off bumpers,
and dialed our anxiety down seventy percent,

altering its tonality
like a pair of strong sunglasses.
We wedged our faces into cereal boxes

and studied silver slivers on cardboard,
careful not to lift our chins
and look directly at the sun.

Part V: Nomadic

Travel

This time around we notice more—the smell
of French toast on the eighth floor, herringbone tiles
in the stairwell. Once out of the hotel we lift our faces
to garlic, cement, espresso, diesel,
slices of scent like crepe ribbon cut loose
and riding the breeze. We even sense
complex aromas—

smoldering genius, a cup full of pennies,
long lines at museums, secret needs—
that tint the very oxygen of the city.
We breathe it all in and walk briskly, relishing the way
dawn spills the world onto us
with a hydraulic groan,

unloading dirt and dazzle from the previous day.
As travelers, we focus on what clings—
gum that won't wash away but spots the sidewalks black,
and freshly hosed gutters holding sticks and bugs
and oil in iron grates
like bits of dark gold sifted from a river.

Memory

Tower of London, WWI centennial, 2014

Acres of ceramic poppies surround the castle.
I heard they took weeks to plant.

They're brilliant for a moment brief as life,
spilling over the wall, flooding the moat,

a river of red for color-thirsty visitors.
In our black travel clothes, we press together

and gaze down at a flow of crimson so audacious
it bleeds through our tendency to forget.

A few days later, we wedge our way in again
to watch volunteers pick the poppies

and lay them back in their boxes.
They labor with backs bent

like Millet's peasant women.
The poppies ebb; the muddy swath widens.

Far from Home

The house on the corner had stacks of comics,
plates of Oreos, glass after glass of grape juice.

My friend had pale skin and purple teeth,
a doll with hair that grew and a bedroom

with a view of the school.
Afternoons, I visited her kitchen table

to forestall the long walk home, lodging myself
in the smell of cartoon ink and the dizzy spill of plots

and characters so facile you could hear the laugh track.
Under the spell of sugar and pablum, I grew dull.

I sponged cookies, thumbed Archies
and skedaddled by nightfall, soul sickened and ready

for the mile-long climb back to the acrid comfort
of squabbling sisters, library books, green vegetables.

A Market in Bristol

Down the street from a half-filled cider glass,
soles scuff cobblestones, and men in aprons sweep
to fill the cracks with last night's adventures.

Their brooms propel us toward the old market.
We teeter up cratered steps to the square,
then past stalls of textiles, records, hats, to where

Moroccan vendors have been cooking tagines
all morning. The crowd ripples to the aroma.
They linger like pigeons and,

when the food finally appears, set to folding fat
ribbons of pita around chunks of carrot and lamb.
Even the drizzle here tastes of paprika.

Our sweaters thick with cinnamon and saffron,
the three of us perch on round seats, tuck knapsacks
between our feet and let the food steam our faces.

As we elbow the mosaic table and revere our lentils,
birds up high, watching for crumbs,
settle on arches of iron.

Camping with Quilts

One to soften roots and rocks
and catch the moisture underneath;
two on top to keep dreams from escaping.

Morning time, you spread the damp quilts on the car
to sweeten in the sun,
let them drape till they're metal-hot and way past dry.

While they steam, you curl in a butterfly chair,
sipping grainy coffee,
warmed inside out by quilt logic.

Off the back hatch hang stripes and cherries,
floral and plaid, white and paisley, sober and gaudy
mismatched squares set in strips like calendar weeks

and stacked, a queen-sized textile month
whose single days confound up close,
but in aggregate they shine.

New Orleans Hosts a History Conference

Shoes smack a flurry of taps; jug band thumps in a corner;
couples sprinkled in powdered sugar float from cafés.

Cigarettes idle and suit jackets swarm; a pack of stilettos
bumps hems higher in a giggling rush between bars,

and through the pleasure-seeking masses, historians cut
a path. Padded with messenger bags, they walk

in a cloud of sentences and sift ideas.
We catch sound clips as we pass—

"She used the category of gender in really essentializing ways"
—beelining through the syncopated banter of Bourbon Street.

A guy in a long wool coat shouts
"We have naked whores! We have beautiful girls!"

to the historians in their zippered jackets, who perk up
and launch a discussion of prostitution in ancient Rome.

Ithaca, NY

On the porch, we crones knit and cackle about a floppy hat.
Whitecaps crash the lake but I sit, anchored

by coffee and yarn, and contemplate staying this time.
I have a scheme. I say I'm making a tea towel, but ten rows in

I unravel it, wind it around the skein and start again.
Driving up from Troy to Ithaca, I felt a long sigh coming

but vented it in dribs and drabs, and the gods didn't notice.
Past a slope on the left, past a ripple on the right, past a far white

silo, I let out spoonfuls of air. When we sidetracked
the uphill forest I exhaled *Hello. Hello maples.*

The cabin was still there but collapsed in a wreckage of
shingles and pink stuffing. I dreamt once

I roped myself to a nearby trunk in the black pit of night
while a high wind shuffled the branches.

Now I recall the body language of trees. I open my lungs
and gust, and the bark absorbs my breezes.

Tropical Wanderer

Oh, Moses, so close yet so far and stuck
with a band of cranky hikers for forty years.

I too want to see the periwinkle blue, the streams of gold,
and even more the pumpkin, saffron, papaya forests

blazing in fall—but all the jobs are here in Florida,
land of the monotone palm tree.

My friends post photos on Facebook of leaves turning,
painful glimpses of the fury of color

we'll miss but our kids will savor
when—by divine forecast—

they finally move to New England.
But our children don't dream of autumn,

have never seen apples stomped into cider or smelled
the first fireplace smoke of the season.

Let's leave the next generation on the precipice,
munching manna, gazing at sunrise over far Canaan

while we old folks venture back there, sweaters in hand.
You know, Mo, God's a tease, a flasher of promises,

the mischief maker who gave us longing
but also suitcases and trains.

Montana

As far as she was concerned, Vermont
was training wheels for Montana.
I've seen recent photos of her
bundled up and blissed out, hugging a horse.

The towns back east crammed her view
with fiddle tunes and muscle pain,
organic bread and poverty,
all-night dances and heartache

and those green bumps on the horizon
made the sky too small.
She wanted to take a full breath at night
under stars flung from one range

to the next. She wanted to
cross an empty plain in the morning,
blink the sun out of her eyes
and take in the dry, high-def air.

Stuck in the brick shadows
of winter solstice, she talked about
the unfenced wide blue of Montana,
and we sang our cowgirl songs.

Souvenir from a Windy Planet

We've landed in a microclimate of shrubs and yucca
with no tall trees to break the wind.

I turn my head and the air's a flag flapping,
turn the other way and grasses *hiss,*

quiet as a lisp. I'd like to let a gust blow in one ear and out
the other and take language with it,

yet still bring home a poem. The guys hike down
into the wash and up on a golden slope.

No one will mind, they said before jumping out of the car,
but I stayed a minute to see what we were up against—

as it turned out, just slashed paths from an old mine,
not a soul or cow in sight.

So I yell, *Stop, so I can take a picture,* but the bluster
grabs my request, shreds it, and sends it over black branches

and rolling land, out to the mountain-ringed horizon.
I want my family posed against the landscape, close-up.

My husband's rust-colored trousers are the same shade
as that pile of tailings, his beard the silver of cholla bones;

my son is brown topped like a rock baked in the sun.
I pick through brambles and crest the hill, where they've already

built a cairn. The three of us look down to chunks of stone,
low plants, a few cacti, all in a planet of pale yellow

that waves beyond the corners of our eyes.
Hair whips my cheeks and tangles against my nose.

I have a barrette, but I won't use it. I'll let my tresses
blow to string so that back home, in the still indoors,

they'll *shush* like dried grass.

About the Author

Sarah Carleton writes poetry, edits fiction, tutors English, plays the banjo, raises her son, and makes her husband laugh in Tampa, Florida. Her poems have appeared in numerous publications, including *Off the Coast, The Binnacle, Cider Press Review, Nimrod, Chattahoochee Review, Tar River Poetry, Crab Orchard Review,* and *New Ohio Review.* This is her first book of poetry.